LIFE
Beyond
DEATH

LIFE *Beyond* DEATH

ROBERT L. MILLET

DESERET BOOK

SALT LAKE CITY, UTAH

ISBN 978-1-62972-920-6

Printed in the United States of America
PubLitho, Draper, UT

10   9   8   7   6   5   4   3   2   1

My wife Shauna's father grew up as an active, involved Latter-day Saint. Somehow through the years, however, he lost the faith he once had and became indifferent toward God and religion. He was in many ways a wonderful man who loved his family and seemed to be a friend to everyone who came to know him. He was a good man. Not long before he died, Shauna tried to describe to me the awful pain she felt in her heart for her dad. I asked if the pain was because he had not enjoyed the blessings of the gospel in his life for so many years. She nodded yes, but there was something even more serious that haunted her: her father didn't believe in life after death. The ache she felt in her soul was that her dad was persuaded that when he breathed his last breath on earth, his existence would come to an end. From his perspective, he would cease to be. It was her father's sense of emptiness, his lack of belief in the immortality of the soul, that weighed upon Shauna's heart. The one consolation she had was that when he did die, he would learn otherwise very quickly.

"All men know they must die," the Prophet Joseph Smith explained. "And it is important that we should understand the reasons and causes of our exposure to the vicissitudes of life and of death, and the designs and purposes of God in our coming into the world, our sufferings here, and our departure hence. . . . *It is but reasonable to suppose that God would reveal something in reference to the matter, and it is a subject we ought to study more than any other. . . .* If we have any claim on our Heavenly Father for anything, it is for knowledge on this important subject."[1]

THE REALITY OF DEATH

There is nothing more common to this life than death; it is the common lot of all who come into this life to leave it. Every man or woman is born, and every man or woman must die. All are born as helpless infants, and all depart this our second estate equally helpless in the face of death. Even among those who read by the lamp of gospel understanding, death is frequently viewed with fear and trembling. President Wilford Woodruff "referred to a saying of Joseph Smith, which he heard him utter (like this), That if the people knew what was behind the veil, they would try by every means to . . . get there. But *the Lord in his wisdom had implanted the fear of death in every person that they might cling to life and thus accomplish the designs of their Creator.*"[2]

Strictly speaking, there is no death and there are no dead. When things die, they do not cease to be; they merely cease to be in this world. Life goes on. Death is a transition, a change in assignment, a transfer to another realm. When we die, our spirit continues to see and act and feel and associate; it is only the physical body that becomes inactive and lifeless for a season. And so it is that we use a term—*death*—to describe what seems to be from our limited perspective. From an eternal vantage point, however, there is only life.

When we speak of a person's "untimely death," we generally mean that it is untimely for us—for those who remain behind.[3] Though it is true that individuals may hasten their death and thus shorten their day of probation,[4] for the faithful there is nothing untimely about death. In speaking at the funeral of Elder Richard L. Evans of the Quorum of the Twelve Apostles, President Joseph Fielding Smith stated: "May I say for the consolation of those who mourn, and for the comfort and guidance of all of us, that no righteous man is ever taken before his time. In the case of the faithful Saints, they are simply transferred to other fields of labor. The Lord's work goes on in this life, in the world of spirits, and in the kingdoms of glory where men go after their resurrection."[5]

Losing family members to death is particularly painful, and members of The Church of Jesus Christ of Latter-day Saints are not spared such feelings. "Thou shalt live together in love," we are instructed in a modern revelation, "insomuch that thou shalt weep for the loss of them that die" (Doctrine and Covenants 42:45). "Irrespective of age," President Russell M. Nelson pointed out, "we mourn for those loved and lost. It is a natural response in complete accord with divine commandment [Doctrine and Covenants 42:45, above]. Moreover, we can't fully appreciate joyful reunions later without tearful separations now." Then this modern prophet put forward a profound truth: "*The only way to take sorrow out of death is to take love out of life.*"[6]

Indeed, we weep and we long for a reassociation, but we do not, as the Apostle Paul wrote, grieve like those who have no hope (see 1 Thessalonians 4:13), for to do so is to express a lack of faith in the purposes and plan of God and to ignore the divine promise of restoration and reunion. "At funerals, our tears are genuine," Elder Neal A. Maxwell observed, "but not because of termination—rather because of interruption. Though just as wet, our tears are not of despair but are of appreciation and anticipation. Yes, for disciples, *the closing of a grave is but the closing of a door which later will be flung open with rejoicing.*"[7]

To be sure, life's bitter winters may find us walking alone. During these cold and dark seasons of solitude, we wrap ourselves in the protective clothing of faith—which faith brings a grand and glorious perspective—and we are warmed by precious memories. Thus we move on, seeking always to view things as God views them. "Precious in the sight of the Lord," the Psalmist declared, "is the death of his saints" (Psalm 116:15). We have the assurance from modern revelation that "those that die shall rest from all their labors, and their works shall follow them; and they shall receive a crown in the mansions of my Father, which I have prepared for them" (Doctrine and Covenants 59:2).

The cycle of life continues everlastingly. If there were no death, there would be no life. If there were no death, then the growth and development and expansion that lie ahead would be forever withheld from us. There is purpose in life, and there is purpose in death. He who knows all things orchestrates the events of our lives and knows what is best for us. Truly, as President Russell M. Nelson pointed out, "we live to die and we die to live—in another realm. If we are well prepared, death brings no terror."[8]

While it is natural and appropriate to weep and mourn for those who have passed on, it is both helpful and healthy for us to contemplate what our loved one will experience as he or she penetrates the veil. "Even as we feel such loss in our lives," Elder Jeffrey R. Holland noted, "*how joyful it must be for that person, other loved ones, and the Lord Himself to have such a joyful reunion beyond the veil.* Nothing is more 'precious' than a humble, worthy, loving life. How grateful we should be, then, when the Lord will say to such an one, 'Well done, thou good and faithful servant: . . . enter into the joy of thy Lord' (Matthew 25:21). *It is worth letting them go in order for them to behold that face and hear those words.*"[9]

THE WORLD OF SPIRITS

There is never a time when we cease to be. Modern prophets and modern scripture attest that the transition from time into eternity is immediate. As we breathe our last breath, our spirit leaves our physical body and passes directly into the postmortal spirit world. At the funeral for Brother James Adams, Joseph Smith taught: "The spirits of the just are exalted to a greater and more glorious work; hence they are blessed in their departure to the world of spirits. Enveloped in flaming fire, *they are not far from us, and know and understand our thoughts, feelings, and motions*, and are often pained therewith."[10] "Is the spirit world here?" President Brigham Young asked. "It is not beyond the sun, but is on this earth that was organized for the people that have lived and that do and will live upon it."[11] "There is no distance in death," President Boyd K. Packer explained. "The spirit world we know is here around us, but the veil is there, and the curtain is there. On occasions we can see and on more occasions we can feel those who have gone beyond."[12]

At the time of one's entrance into the spirit world, the person experiences what President Joseph F. Smith called a "partial judgment."[13] He or she goes either to paradise or to what the prophets have variously called spirit prison, hell, or outer darkness (see 1 Peter 3:18–19; 2 Nephi 9:12; Alma 40:13). Paradise is the abode of the righteous, a state of happiness, "a state of rest, a state of peace, where they shall rest from all their troubles and from all care, and sorrow" (Alma 40:12). Paradise is a place where spirits "expand in wisdom, where they have respite from all their troubles, and where care and sorrow do not annoy."[14] On the other hand, the spirits of the wicked "shall be cast out into outer darkness; there shall be weeping, and wailing, and gnashing of teeth, and this because of their own iniquity, being led captive by the will of the devil" (Alma 40:13).

Modern revelation also makes clear that the entire spirit world, not just that portion known as hell or outer darkness, is, in a sense, a "spirit prison."[15] Though there are divisions of some kind between the righteous and the wicked, all of the spirits of men and women are in one world, just as they are in our earthly life. In the postmortal spirit world, the disembodied long for deliverance, seek for relief from their disembodied condition, and look upon the long absence of their spirits from their bodies as a bondage (see Doctrine and Covenants 45:17; 138:50). "When our spirits leave these bodies, will they be happy?" Elder Orson Pratt asked. "Not perfectly so," he answered. "Why? Because the spirit is absent from the body; it cannot be perfectly happy while a part of the man is lying in the earth. . . . You will be happy, you will be at ease in paradise; but still you will be looking for a house where your spirit can enter and act as you did in former times."[16]

The Apostle Peter declared that Jesus went, after His mortal death, to preach to the "spirits in prison" (1 Peter 3:19; see verses 18, 20). We know from latter-day revelation that the Master did not minister in person to the wicked (see Doctrine and Covenants 138:20–22, 29, 37)—Jesus preached to the spirits in prison in the sense that He preached the gospel in the spirit world. More specifically, "from among the righteous [in paradise], he organized his forces and appointed messengers, clothed with power and authority, and commissioned them to go forth and carry the light of the gospel to them that were in darkness, even to all the spirits of men" (Doctrine and Covenants 138:30).

Just as there are variations among the godly in paradise, so also there are differences among those in hell or spirit prison. There are the very wicked who, as Alma explained, are subject to confrontation, suffering, and repentance. There are others—good people, honorable men and women (see Doctrine and Covenants 76:75)—who have not enjoyed the blessings of the fulness of the gospel because such were unavailable to them. These people work and grow and learn and develop. Many of them open their hearts to the gospel message and are taught. "The gospel is preached to the ignorant, the unrepentant, and the rebellious," President Dallin H. Oaks pointed out, "so they can be freed from their bondage and go forward to the blessings a loving Heavenly Father has in store for them."[17]

Modern prophets have further clarified that once the gospel message is delivered and accepted by individuals in the spirit world, and when the appropriate ordinances have been performed by those in the flesh who act as proxy for the departed, "the Lord has administrators there to set them free."[18] That is, once a person has received the gospel and its saving ordinances, he or she is permitted to cross that gulf that separates hell from paradise and thereafter enjoy sweet association with the faithful (see Luke 16:26; see also 1 Nephi 15:28–30).[19]

In the meridian of time, the Apostle Peter taught the Saints scattered abroad that all persons will eventually give an accounting "to him that is ready to judge the quick and the dead. For for this cause was the gospel preached also to them that are dead, *that they might be judged according to men in the flesh, but live according to God in the spirit*" (1 Peter 4:5–6; emphasis added). Knowing the goodness and justice of our God, we do not suppose that it would be any easier to accept the gospel as a disembodied spirit than it is in mortality. And yet, in our fallen telestial world there are so many factors that can bear upon a person's capacity to see, hear, feel, understand, and receive the truth. Indeed, as we approach the great millennial day, the index of moral pollution will rise, thus making it more and more difficult to remain unscathed and unwounded in the war against evil. "It is my conviction," President Boyd K. Packer testified, "that those wicked influences one day will be overruled."[20]

"In this space between death and the resurrection of the body," President Joseph F. Smith has instructed us, "the two classes of souls remain, in happiness or in misery, until the time which is appointed of God that the dead shall come forth and be reunited both spirit and body."[21] Thus the postmortal spirit world is an intermediate stop for all men and women. It is a place of waiting, of repentance and suffering, of peace and rest, and of instruction and preparation. Those who receive and enjoy the blessings of the gospel (celestial) or who at least receive the testimony of Jesus (terrestrial) will come forth from the spirit world in the First Resurrection, the Resurrection of the just (see Doctrine and Covenants 76:51, 74, 82). Those who continue to assert their own will[22] and refuse the Savior's message of salvation, including His offer of cleansing and renewal, will remain in the spirit world until the thousand years are ended. These will then take part in that Second or Last Resurrection and come forth, either to a telestial glory or to a kingdom of no glory (see Doctrine and Covenants 76:32–44; 88:24, 32).

No one leaves this world perfectly pure and without flaw. The work of spiritual refinement and transformation, accomplished through the atoning blood of Jesus Christ and the sanctifying work of the Holy Spirit, continues for each one of us as we enter the world of spirits.[23] President Dallin H. Oaks reminded the Latter-day Saints that "modern revelation reveals that the work of salvation goes forward in the spirit world (see Doctrine and Covenants 138:30–34, 58), and although we are urged not to procrastinate our repentance during mortality (see Alma 13:27), we are taught that some repentance is possible there."[24]

I recall very clearly the stirring words of President Boyd K. Packer, delivered at the funeral for his beloved apostolic colleague, Elder Bruce R. McConkie. Having spoken of Elder McConkie's remarkable ministry and of his distinctive and very direct way of preaching the gospel, President Packer asked: "Where is Bruce McConkie now? He is with his Lord. *When the refining process is complete, I know something of how he will appear. He will be glorious!* What will he do? Whatever the Lord wills him to do. I believe he shall be, as the revelation describes them, 'a chosen messenger, clothed with power and authority to go forth and carry the light of the gospel to them that [are] in darkness.'"[25]

"THIS DAY . . . IN PARADISE"

On the cross of Calvary, Jesus hung between two thieves. One of them "railed on him, saying, If thou be Christ [the Messiah], save thyself and us. But the other answering rebuked him, saying, Dost not thou fear God, seeing thou art in the same condemnation? And we indeed justly; for we receive the due reward of our deeds: but this man hath done nothing amiss. And he said unto Jesus, Lord, remember me when thou comest into thy kingdom. And Jesus said unto him, Verily I say unto thee, To day shalt thou be with me in paradise" (Luke 23:39–43).

As we might expect, this passage has given rise to a whole host of interpretations. Many Christians believe that the thief was promised that he would enter heaven once he died, or from a Latter-day Saint perspective, would be welcomed into the celestial kingdom. As one might suppose, such an interpretation opens the doctrinal door to a belief in a kind of "deathbed repentance." To be sure, it is good to repent, no matter when we do it. That is, it is better to repent than to remain in our sins. The Prophet Joseph Smith taught, "There is never a time when the spirit is too old to approach God. All are within the reach of pardoning mercy, who have not committed the unpardonable sin."[26]

While we would never denigrate the value of sincere repentance—no matter how late in one's mortal probation (see Matthew 20:1–16)—we must acknowledge the divine word that "he that repents *and does the commandments of the Lord* shall be forgiven" (Doctrine and Covenants 1:32; emphasis added). The Savior affirmed: "Not every one that saith unto me, Lord, Lord, shall enter into the kingdom of heaven; but he that doeth the will of my Father which is in heaven" (Matthew 7:21).

The Prophet Joseph taught on one occasion that "the infidel will grasp at every straw for help until death stares him in the face, and then his infidelity takes its flight, for the realities of the eternal world are resting upon him in mighty power; and when every earthly support and prop fails him, he then sensibly feels the eternal truths of the immortality of the soul. We should take warning and not wait for the death-bed to repent. . . . Let this, then, prove as a warning to all not to procrastinate repentance, or wait till a death-bed, for it is the will of God that man should repent and serve him in health, and in the strength and power of his mind, in order to secure his blessing, and not wait until he is called to die."[27]

Further, we must look a little deeper into this matter in order to understand what the Savior really said to the thief on the cross. Did the Master actually promise the thief that he would, at the time of death, enter into paradise, the realm of the righteous? New Testament scholar N. T. Wright has written: "'Today you will be with me in paradise.' There will still, of course, be a future completion involving ultimate resurrection; Luke's overall theological understanding leaves no doubt on that score. Jesus, after all, didn't rise again 'today,' that is, on Good Friday. Luke must have understood him to be referring to a state . . . *prior to the resurrection*." Wright went on to conclude that resurrection "was, in other words, life *after* life after death."[28]

"I will say something about the spirits in prison," the Prophet Joseph taught. "There has been much said by modern divines about the words of Jesus (when on the cross) to the thief, saying, 'This day shalt thou be with me in paradise.' King James' translators make it out to say paradise. But what is paradise? It is a modern word: it does not answer at all to the original word that Jesus made use of [presumably the word *hades*]. Find the original of the word paradise. You might as easily find a needle in a haymow. . . . There is nothing in the original word in Greek from which this was taken that signifies paradise; but it was—*This day thou shalt be with me in the world of spirits*: then I will teach you all about it and answer your inquiries."[29]

WHEN PEOPLE TAKE THEIR OWN LIVES

Now just a word about those who die by their own choice, that is, those who die by suicide. There are few moments in our mortal existence when we need to be so completely nonjudgmental than when a loved one or dear friend dies in this manner. Our Lord and Savior counsels us in His Sermon on the Mount to "Judge not unrighteously, that ye be not judged; but judge righteous judgment" (JST, Matthew 7:2).

President Dallin H. Oaks explained that each of us must make judgments every day of our lives. We must decide whether we will attend a particular social event, violate the Sabbath day, watch that questionable video, contribute to a gossip session, or continue to be a part of a friendship or association that is far more destructive to us than helpful. These are what President Oaks called *intermediate* judgments, matters that we need to decide here and now. Indeed, we *must* make such judgments. Our spiritual lives depend upon us doing so. What our Master warns against is what President Oaks called *final* judgments. He taught that we "presume to make final judgments whenever we proclaim that any particular person is going to hell (or to heaven) for a particular act or at a particular time. When we do this—and there is great temptation to do so—we hurt ourselves and the person we pretend to judge."

He also stated: "We must refrain from making judgments on people, because we lack the knowledge and wisdom to do so. We would even apply the wrong standards. The world's way is to judge competitively between winners and losers. The Lord's way of final judgment will be to apply His perfect knowledge of the law a person has received and to judge on the basis of that person's circumstances, motives, and actions throughout his or her entire life."[30]

You and I have no idea what is going on within other people's minds and hearts; what pressures and challenges they are facing; what heavy burdens they are carrying; what pain and suffering and anguish fills their daily lives; what hopes and dreams are being stifled and blocked by mental, emotional, or physical tests. Only an omniscient and omni-loving God can and does know such things. With such persons we assume the best and we hope and pray for the best.

So many of our Father's children have been subjected to much of pain and distress in their lives, to abuse, to neglect, to the agonies of wanting more than anything to live a normal life and to feel normal feelings, but who seem unable to do so.

Each one of us, whoever we are, wrestles with something. To some extent at least, many have their own "thorn in the flesh" like the Apostle Paul (2 Corinthians 12:7; see verses 8–10). Perhaps it's struggles or challenges that pass in time. Perhaps it's the torture of watching helplessly as loved ones choose unwisely and thereby close doors of opportunity for themselves. And then there are the terrible traumas in our lives, those occasions when someone we love violates our tender trust and deals a blow that strikes at the center of all we hold dear and all we value about ourselves. I have a conviction that the day is coming when all the wrongs, the awful wrongs of this life, will be righted. The God of justice and mercy will see to that.

I believe that when a person passes through the veil of death, all those impediments and challenges and crosses that were beyond his or her power to face or control will be lifted from his or her mind and heart, and then peace will prevail. In speaking specifically of those who have taken their lives, Elder Robert D. Hales has written, "In all matters of individual salvation, I take great hope in the knowledge that all of us will be judged by the Savior, who knows our circumstances perfectly. . . . *We may be surprised at just how much mercy will be available from the Savior*, who was 'made like unto his brethren, that he might be a merciful and faithful high priest' (Hebrews 2:17)."[31]

President M. Russell Ballard offered these significant insights: "I feel that judgment for sin is not always as cut-and-dried as some of us seem to think. The Lord said, 'Thou shalt not kill.' Does that mean that every person who kills will be condemned, no matter the circumstances? Civil law recognizes that there are gradations in this matter—from accidental manslaughter to self-defense to first-degree murder. I feel that the Lord also recognizes differences in intent and circumstances: Was the person who took his life mentally ill? Was he or she so deeply depressed as to be unbalanced or otherwise emotionally disturbed? Was the suicide a tragic, pitiful call for help that went unheeded too long or progressed faster than the victim intended? Did he or she somehow not understand the seriousness of the act? Was he or she suffering from a chemical imbalance that led to despair and a loss of self-control? . . . Obviously, we do not know the full circumstances surrounding every suicide. Only the Lord knows all the details, and he it is who will judge our actions here on earth."[32]

THE VEIL IS THIN

My testimony and my experience teach me that the veil that separates us from the postmortal spirit world is thin. Occasionally, when necessary and in keeping with the laws of the spirit world, beloved family members and friends on the other side—seen and unseen—minister to those who live on this side. They do not cease to love us when they depart this life, nor do they cease to care for us, or, in some cases, to minister in our behalf. In speaking of those family members or close associates who have finished their work in mortality, President Joseph F. Smith explained that "we live in their presence, they see us, they are solicitous for our welfare, they love us now more than ever. For now they see the dangers that beset us; . . . They see the temptations and the evils that beset us in life . . . hence their solicitude for us, and their love for us, and their desire for our well being, must be greater than that which we feel for ourselves."[33]

My sister-in-law Sherrie (Shauna's sister) suffered with a blood disease for many years. She received special injections regularly to build up her blood. After twelve years, however, the injections no longer had an effect. At that point, her physicians discovered that she had leukemia and recommended that she begin chemotherapy. Sherrie did some serious thinking and praying and decided that she would forego chemo and continue in her remaining time on earth with some quality of life. At that point she was informed that she had very little time to live. She was placed on hospice care.

Sherrie lived in a downstairs apartment in the home of her son Darrin and his wife Jamie. She was doing quite well until December of 2016. At this point she began to suffer a great deal of pain, and the hospice nurse suggested that she not be left alone. Jamie and Darrin took time off work to stay with her. My wife Shauna was scheduled to spend time with her also the week after Christmas. On the 26th of December, Sherrie fell as a result of her weakened condition, and paramedics were called in to help get her back into bed. By 11:00 p.m. that night, Sherrie was settled into bed. Jamie asked the hospice nurse if someone should stay with her mother-in-law for the rest of the night, but the nurse recommended that they get some sleep, since they were at this point physically spent. Besides, the nurse pointed out, Sherrie was exhausted as well and would probably sleep. A baby monitor had been placed in her room to pick up any sounds should Sherrie need assistance.

As Darrin and Jamie were leaving her room, they overheard Sherrie say, "Oh, Mom, help me. Please help me!" They then went to bed themselves. At 3:00 a.m., Darrin went downstairs to check on his mother and found that she had passed away. The hospice nurse explained that Sherrie had died about two hours earlier. No one in the family doubted but that Sherrie's and Shauna's mother, who had been in the spirit world herself since 2004, did in fact come to her daughter as the moment arrived for Sherrie to leave mortality. It was a sweet and tender reminder that, on both sides of the veil, parents never cease to love and care for their children, and that the family is the most important unit in time or eternity.

My father was a wonderful man who loved his children and his grandchildren. He did all he could to assist us while he was alive, although in the closing decade of his life he wrestled with one physical ailment after another. Without question, his greatest impact on my family—which, of course, is his family, too—has come since he has passed through the veil of death and been allowed to minister on occasion to loved ones. If the reader will indulge me, I'd like to share a couple of personal experiences that illustrate just how close we are to those who have passed into the next world.

Many years ago, one of our children chose to leave the fold

and separate, not only from Church activity but also from family association. He became heavily involved with addictive substances and managed to bury himself in a hellish world that held out little hope for normal living in the future. Shauna and I had prayed and wrestled and yearned for his recovery and return, but we had heard nothing and were left to wonder whether he was dead, imprisoned, or lost. The burden of pain and awful anticipation of a notification of incarceration or drug overdose grew heavier each day. One night as Shauna and I knelt in prayer, broken and torn emotionally and physically weak from worry, we wept through our prayers and pleaded long and hard, once again, for the Good Shepherd to lead our wandering sheep home.

Sometime during that night, I found myself dreaming. My father, who had passed away in March of 1988, came to me in the dream, embraced me, and then looked me in the eye and said quite forcefully: "Son, I want you to pull yourself together. I am going to help you with those children of yours. Be patient." I awoke and immediately sat up in bed. The holy presence I felt attested to me that what I had just received was heaven-sent.

My sudden movement awoke Shauna, and she asked: "What's wrong? What happened?" I explained that I had seen Dad in a dream and that he told me he planned to help with our children. Shauna and I both began to cry as deep feelings of gratitude and reassurance flowed into our souls. Only days later the phone rang during the middle of the night. Our son said: "I just can't live like this anymore.

Can I come home?" We were so thrilled to hear from him, so grateful to know that he was still alive, that we felt no need to set the terms or specify under what conditions he could return. We simply welcomed him home with love and affection.

A few weeks later my son and I were sitting on the sofa in the living room one evening. He turned to me and said hesitantly, "Dad, I need to share something with you." I nodded and encouraged him to proceed. He said: "I know this sounds strange, but one night a while back I was on the verge of doing something terrible that would definitely have cost me my life. I then heard Grandpa Millet's voice call me by name and say: 'Don't do that! You have been taught better. Now get up and go home.' Dad, is that too weird to be true?" my son asked.

With some emotion I said that it definitely was not weird, and added, "Now I have a story to tell you." I then told of my dream. We felt the Spirit of the Lord resting upon us, knew that the entire experience was divinely orchestrated, and embraced.

My youngest brother, Ron, passed away long before he should have. He struggled with life and could never quite discover who he was or why he was on earth. Tragically, in his quest for some level of happiness, he seemed always to be looking in all the wrong places and associating with all the wrong people. He stumbled throughout most of his short thirty-eight years on earth, ever reaching for telestial toys that brought him no lasting satisfaction. Our family loved him dearly and prayed for him constantly, but none of us seemed to be able to penetrate the spiritual wall he had constructed over decades. At about age thirty-six he contracted AIDS, probably from unclean needles he had used to inject himself with drugs.

In his last year and as he faced death, he became much more sober—his feelings were close to the surface, and the pull of his addictions seemed to diminish. Because he lived with my mother in Louisiana, I was not able to see him very often, but when I was with him I tried to discuss things that matter most. He listened. He grieved painfully over the fact that he had wasted most of his time on the earth. He asked many questions about life after death and the world to come, and I did my best to provide answers, at least on those matters about which the prophets have spoken. This was an especially difficult time for my mother, who said more than once that "it's not right for a mother to have to bury her children." Thankfully Ron slipped away quietly and peacefully. We held the funeral services, but Mom was almost inconsolable. My dad had passed away many years before, and so he could not be with her, at least on this side of the veil.

Just a word about my father. He was quite an athlete in his day. As a high school football player, he was an all-state quarterback and then played college ball for a time with Louisiana State University. Even many years later when I was a young boy, Dad continued to compete in a basketball league. I can still picture him in my mind leading fast breaks down the court. But his real love was football, and

Dad and I spent many hours tossing the ball or watching his beloved LSU Tigers on television.

My mom and I sat at the gravesite and listened as a dear friend dedicated the grave and offered words of consolation. Mom turned to me at a certain point and said, "I'm so afraid that Ronnie will be all alone, with no one to take care of him." I tried to explain briefly that she had no reason to fear—that God loved her son even more than we did. Then, after a few moments, and without warning, I heard a voice, one I have come to recognize through the years. It was my father's voice. He had a message he needed to deliver, and he did just that.

As we walked away from the grave toward our car, I struggled to hold back the emotions I was feeling. I whispered to Mom that there was something I needed to tell her, and she asked what it was. I said, as nearly as I can recollect, "Mama, you don't need to worry about Ronnie anymore. I just heard Dad's voice."

"What did he say?" she responded with wide eyes and eagerness.

I replied, "He said, 'It's a handoff. I'll take him from here.'"

For the first time in days, a tender smile graced Mom's face. She embraced me and said, "Oh, I am so relieved."

Dad knew a lot about handoffs, as he had delivered the football into the hands of his running backs, many, many times. But that day a different kind of handoff took place: Mom's youngest son, my younger brother, was welcomed into the spirit world by my affectionate and ever-solicitous father. Now we both knew for certain that

Ron would not be alone, that someone who loved him a great deal would be with him. Her tears dried up, and peace rested upon our family for many days.

CONCLUSION

With the restoration of divine truths concerning life after death, light has replaced darkness, sound doctrine has replaced ignorance and superstition, and men and women can now travel the covenant path without that ominous fear of what follows death. Latter-day prophets have taught us where we came from, why we are here, and where we are going when death calls to each of us, when we pass through that veil that separates time and eternity.

Perhaps you have recently lost a loved one or a trusted friend. Maybe you or someone you care about deeply are facing an imminent death. To all of us, no matter our rank or station in life, no matter our present state of health or sickness, the testimony of God's prophets resounds: Life goes on when we depart this second estate. You and I will retain our identity. The love and fellowship and brother- and sisterhood we have enjoyed throughout our mortal lives has not come to an end; it has only been interrupted for a season. The Prophet of the Restoration spoke comforting words when he declared: "When the Savior shall appear we shall see him as he is. We shall see that he is a man like ourselves. And *that same sociality which exists among us here will exist among us there, only it will be coupled with eternal glory, which glory we do not now enjoy*" (Doctrine and Covenants 130:1–2; emphasis added).

All of this is possible because our Father in Heaven loves us. Indeed, He loves us so much that He sent His Only Begotten Son into the world, that we might have an abundant life here and life eternal hereafter (see John 3:16; 10:10). I bear witness that in Christ there is peace. In Christ there is hope—hope for deliverance from sin and death, hope for salvation and exaltation. In his own inimitable style, Elder Neal A. Maxwell spoke in one April general conference: "As this Easter day draws to a close, how fitting that we contemplate atoning Jesus—bending and curved in Gethsemane. His bleeding curvature transformed the grammar of death. Until Gethsemane and Calvary, death was a punctuating, rigid exclamation point! Then death, too, curved—into a mere comma!"[34]

I testify that there are no wrongs that will not be righted in time or eternity, no burdens that will not be lifted, no questions that will not eventually be answered. Joseph Smith offered this sweet assurance: "All your losses will be made up to you in the resurrection, provided you continue faithful. By the vision of the Almighty I have seen it."[35] As Christians, let us join with the Apostle Paul in an exultant cry: "Thanks be to God, [who gives] us the victory through our Lord Jesus Christ" (1 Corinthians 15:57; see also John 16:33). May each of us find peace and joy in the soul-stirring realization that life and love and learning are forever.

NOTES

1. Joseph Smith, Journal, 9 October 1843; "Minutes of a Special Conference," *Times and Seasons*, 6 vols. (Nauvoo, IL: The Church of Jesus Christ of Latter-day Saints, 1839–46), 15 September 1843, 4:331; emphasis added.
2. *Diary of Charles L. Walker*, 2 vols., ed. A. Karl Larson and Kathrine Miles Larson (Logan, UT: Utah State University Press, 1980), 1:595–96; emphasis added; spelling and punctuation corrected.
3. "We sometimes speak of death as an 'untimely' death. I suppose that would be true when young people die, when there are families that are pulled apart through accident and difficulties that might be called untimely. But death itself is not. Time is measured only to man, the Lord said. And He said that He can recompense and put things together" (Boyd K. Packer, in *Mine Errand from the Lord: Selections from the Sermons and Writings of Boyd K. Packer*, ed. Clyde J. Williams [Salt Lake City: Deseret Book, 2008], 49).
4. See Spencer W. Kimball, "Tragedy or Destiny?" Brigham Young University devotional address, delivered on 6 December 1955; in *Faith Precedes the Miracle* (Salt Lake City: Deseret Book, 1972), 103–5.
5. Address given at the funeral of Elder Richard L. Evans, 4 November 1971, typescript, 2.
6. "Doors of Death," *Ensign*, May 1992; see also *Teachings of Russell M. Nelson* (Salt Lake City: Deseret Book, 2018), 79–80; emphasis added.
7. "All Hell Is Moved," *1977 Devotional Speeches of the Year* (Provo, UT: Brigham Young University Press, 1978), 181; emphasis added.
8. "Now Is the Time to Prepare," *Ensign*, May 2005; see also *Teachings of Russell M. Nelson*, 77.

9. *For Times of Trouble: Spiritual Solace from the Psalms* (Salt Lake City: Deseret Book, 2010), 121–22; emphasis added.

10. Joseph Smith, Journal, 9 October 1843; "Minutes of a Special Conference," *Times and Seasons*, 15 September 1843, 4:331–32; emphasis added.

11. *Discourses of Brigham Young*, comp. John A. Widtsoe (Salt Lake City: Deseret Book, 1978), 376.

12. *Mine Errand from the Lord*, 47.

13. *Gospel Doctrine* (Salt Lake City: Deseret Book, 1971), 448–49.

14. Joseph F. Smith, *Gospel Doctrine*, 448.

15. See Bruce R. McConkie, "A New Commandment: Save Thyself and thy Kindred!" *Ensign*, August 1976.

16. *Journal of Discourses*, 26 vols. (Liverpool: F. D. Richards & Sons, 1851–86), 1:289–90.

17. "Trust the Lord," *Ensign*, November 2019.

18. Joseph Smith, Discourse, 12 May 1844, Joseph Smith Collection, Church Historian's Library; see also Dallin H. Oaks, "Trust the Lord," *Ensign*, November 2019.

19. See Joseph Fielding Smith, *Doctrines of Salvation*, 3 vols., comp. Bruce R. McConkie (Salt Lake City: Bookcraft, 1954–56), 2:135, 158, 230.

20. "Our Moral Environment," *Ensign*, May 1992.

21. *Gospel Doctrine*, 448.

22. C. S. Lewis perceptively wrote: "There are only two kinds of people in the end: those who say to God, 'Thy will be done,' and those to whom God says, 'Thy will be done.' All that are in Hell, choose it. . . . No soul that seriously and constantly desires joy will ever miss it. Those who seek find. To those who knock it is opened" (*The Great Divorce* [New York: Touchstone, 1996], 72).

23. C. S. Lewis put it this way: Christ "said (in the Bible) that we were 'gods' and He is going to make good His words. If we let Him—for we can prevent Him, if we choose—He will make the feeblest and filthiest of us into a god or a goddess, a dazzling, radiant, immortal creature. . . . The process will be long and in parts very painful; but that is what we are in for. Nothing less. He meant what He said." Lewis taught further: "*The change will not be completed in this life,*

for death is an important part of the treatment" (*Mere Christianity* [New York: Touchstone, 1996], 176, 177; emphasis added).

24. "Trust the Lord," *Ensign*, November 2019; see also Doctrine and Covenants 138:29–34, 58–59.

25. Funeral held in Salt Lake City on 23 April 1985; in Boyd K. Packer, *Let Not Your Heart Be Troubled* (Salt Lake City: Bookcraft, 1991), 266; emphasis added.

26. Discourse, 3 October 1841 (*Times and Seasons*).

27. Discourse, 20 March 1842. See also Alma 13:27–30; 34:31–35.

28. *Surprised by Hope: Rethinking Heaven, the Resurrection, and the Mission of the Church* (New York: Harper One, 2008), 150–51; emphasis in original.

29. Joseph Smith, Journal, 11 June 1843; Wilford Woodruff Journal, 11 June 1843; emphasis added.

30. "'Judge Not' and Judging," *Ensign*, August 1999; see also *With Full Purpose of Heart* (Salt Lake City: Deseret Book, 2002), 192–93.

31. *Return: Four Phases of Our Mortal Journey Home* (Salt Lake City: Deseret Book, 2010), 408–9; emphasis added.

32. "Suicide," *Ensign*, November 1987.

33. "In the Presence of the Divine," April 1916 general conference; in *Messages of the First Presidency*, 6 vols., comp. James R. Clark (Salt Lake City: Bookcraft, 1965–75), 5:6–7.

34. "The Great Plan of the Eternal God," *Ensign*, May 1984.

35. Joseph Smith, Journal, 16 April 1843.

ABOUT THE AUTHOR

ROBERT L. MILLET, former dean of Religious Education at Brigham Young University, is a professor emeritus of ancient scripture. After receiving bachelor's and master's degrees from BYU in psychology, he earned a PhD from Florida State University in religious studies. Brother Millet is a beloved speaker and the author of numerous books. He and his wife, Shauna, are the parents of six children.